Advance Praise for MY POCKETBOOK

Love this book! Reading it brought back memories of my Mom; she always wanted h... wherever she was, even in the years she had dementia. My Pocketbook is a book to share.

Karen Roller, retired clothing retailer, Gloucester, MA

Susanne Demetri and Karen Gross have written a beautiful story that depicts the importance of transitional objects in childhood and throughout the life cycle. This charming pocketbook book will validate and educate while entertaining people of all ages.

Dr. Donna Friedman, Early Childhood psychologist, NYC

Something really struck me about the story about the pocketbook. It was so relatable to me because my mother never goes anywhere without hers. When I was young, I would search throughout her purse regularly, finding goodies and different receipts. Shiny coins and cases of lipstick ... I learned that something as simple as a pocketbook actually represents much more.

Bunker Hill Community Child Psychology Student, Spring 2022

Karen Gross' books ... leave you hanging on every word. She leaves you wanting more. She always captures you, embraces you, educates you and leaves you with a huge smile on your face with a sense of understanding and total glee...and she gives you her pocketbook!

Jackie Coogan, Adjunct Faculty, Bunker Hill Community College, Spring 2022

MY POCKETBOOK

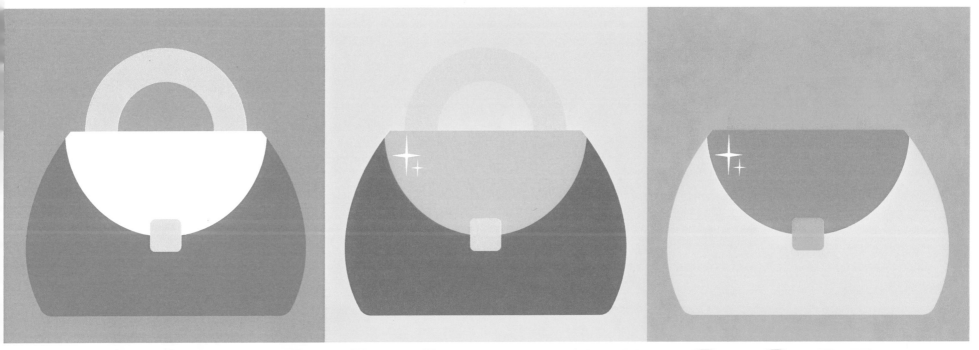

MY POCKETBOOK

By Susanne Demetri and Karen Gross

Published in the United States by LLQ

Teaching tools for this book are available at www.karengrosseducation.com

Library of Congress Cataloging-in-Publication Data is available at loc.gov.

Identifiers:
ISBN 979-8-9862716-1-3 (paperback printed book)
ISBN 979-8-9862716-0-6 (hardcover printed book)
ISBN 979-8-9862716-2-0 (ebook)

Printed on acid-free paper.

Manufactured in the U.S.A.

Book design by Tina Koenig

This story is dedicated to all the girls and boys and women and men who have carried pocketbooks, many of whom do so, we suspect, without knowing why.

Now they can carry them with pride.

Take a photo of your pocketbook and place it below.
Or draw your pocketbook below.

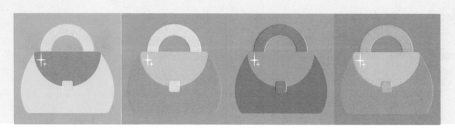

When I was young,
Everybody teased me
Because I always
Had a pocketbook
With me.

I took it with me
When I went outside.

When I went to the store.

When I went to school.

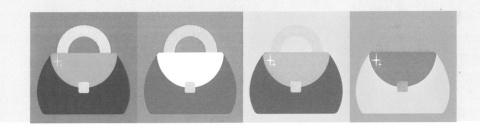

3

I took it to friends' houses.
I took it to sports games.
I took it to my Grandma's house.
I took it on car trips.
I took it everywhere I went.

Sometimes, I even took it to bed
With me.

Other times, it just sat on the night table
Watching over me.

5

Everyone would ask me:
"What's in your pocketbook?
It looks so full."
And I would reply:
"Lots of things. My things."

Sometimes I had crayons in it.
Sometimes I had crackers in it.
Sometimes I had a penny or two in it.
Sometimes I just stuffed it with paper

So it looked all filled up.

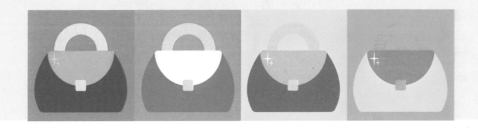

When I was young,
I think my mother emptied my pocketbook
At night or when I wasn't looking.

Because my pocketbook always had room
For new things each day.

She never mentioned it.
She never asked about it.
She just made sure I had room in
My pocketbook for my things.

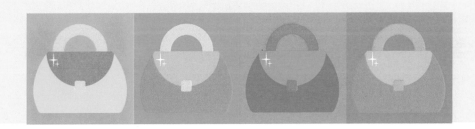

Once, I thought I had lost
My pocketbook and
I was really scared I had left it
Somewhere never to be found
And it was gone, gone, gone.
Gone forever and ever.

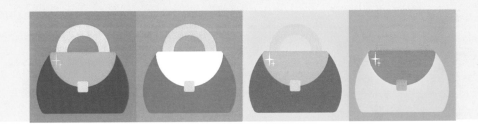

But I found it
Under the covers
Of my bed

Resting there and
Waiting for me.

I think it missed
Being on my arm.

Just as I had
Missed it.

As I grew older, I still carried a pocketbook,
Although I called it a purse then.

That was a way more grown-up way of saying
Pocketbook back then
Although other new words
Have been invented and are used today
Like handbags and man bags.

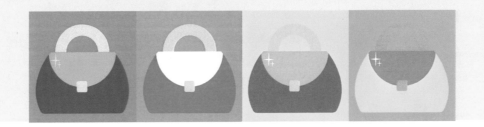

15

When I was a teenager I carried my secret diary
and my pen in it.

I carried a comb and lipstick and keys on a chain in it.

I carried a few dollar bills all crumpled up.

I carried used gum wrappers and pink and white mints
wrapped in plastic.

And sometimes I carried
A photo of my favorite television actor.
(Richard Chamberlain if you are curious.)

I changed my purses to match my clothes
And I had quite a collection of purses.

But, no matter the size or color, I always
Always had a purse with me,
Even though my friends teased me about
My constant wrist friend.

When I was a young mother, I had a big purse
I filled it with toys and snacks
For my children.

I filled it with papers and shopping lists
And reminder notes.

I filled it with schedules.

Sometimes, there was even
An orphaned earring or two.

My purse always had a letter
Or two or three
Some to mail and some
Recently received.

I always had stamps in my purse
Although I could never find them.

They hid, it seemed to me, and never
Wanted to be found.

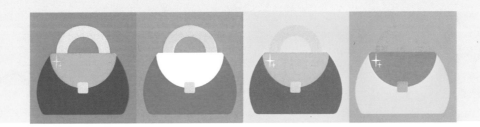

23

And yes, I had coins and paper money
And credit cards and
My driver's license with its
Horrible mugshot-like photo.

I sometimes refused to change purses, even
If the one I was using didn't match
What I was wearing or
Had a hole in it or a
Tattered look.

It was too much work to move things
Or I was stuck doing what
I was doing and sorting
Wasn't my thing.

There was just too much to transfer,
Anyway.

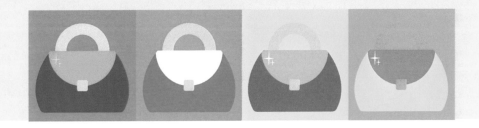

Even when my mother bought
Me a new shiny
Purse to replace my worn-in one,
I didn't use it and it just sat in a
Closet – empty and waiting.

29

As I got older, I still carried a purse.

I carried glasses and tissues and
Life savers and money
And credits cards
And pictures of my grandchildren.

I carried a flip phone that was red
So I could find it easily.

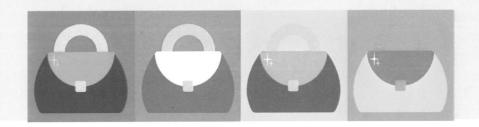

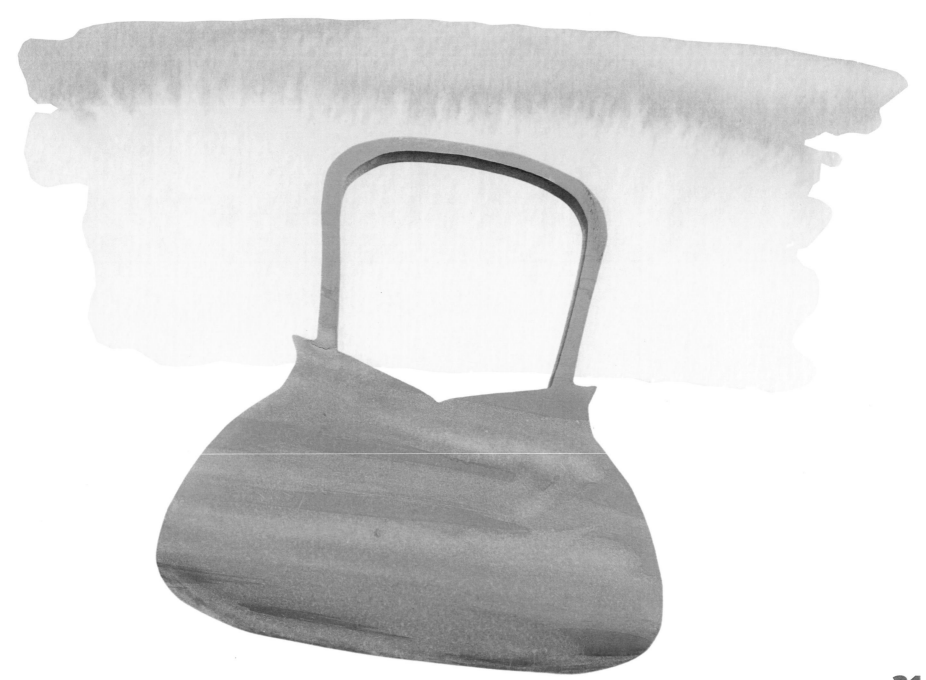

I carried notepads and some pencils.

I carried lists of to-dos and
Business cards – mine and others
And letters and bills to mail.

And I carried the handwritten names
And phone numbers of my
Doctors on a pink index card,
Stuffed in a purse's zipper pocket
just in case.

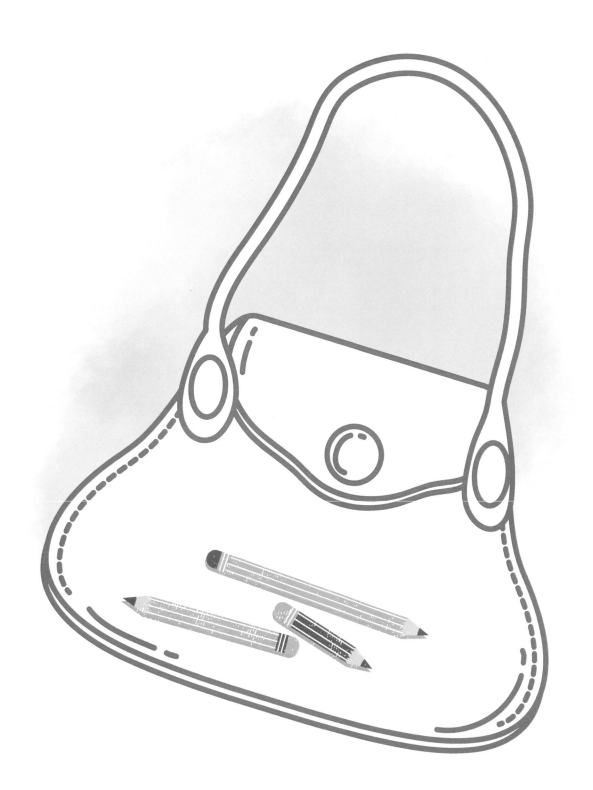

33

Now I am much older and
I don't go out all that much
But I still carry a pocketbook
Wherever I go.

My children and grandchildren
tell me to leave it at home
Or in their car
Because they say that
I don't need it.

They will take care of me
They will pay.
They will buy me what
I want or need.

But I would never leave my purse behind.
It stays with me.

It reminds me of home even when I am far away,
Not that I travel all that much these days.

But wherever I am,
Having my purse with me makes me free to buy something
If I see something special for
Someone or for myself.

And it reminds me to remember
All the things I have carried in my long
Life, some way heavier than others.

Yesterday, my granddaughter came to see me and she saw my pocketbook resting on a table nearby.

She asked if she could look inside and when I said,
"yes," she emptied all its contents on the floor
And as she did, she smiled broadly and said:
"I want a purse too so I can carry
My things with me everywhere I go."

"You might get teased if you do," I said,
"Just like I was teased when I was a young girl."

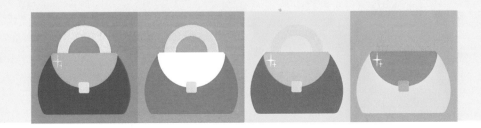

"No worries," she said to me.

"I will tell everyone that
Pocketbooks are magical.

They always help you find
Your way home.

They always help you find your way home."

And so...I gave her one of my favorite pocketbooks
And tucked a wee note inside that said:
"Take me with you, always."

Background

This story is based on a true story and reflects the importance of transitional objects for children and adults alike. As children, we often carry objects with us to help us feel safe, whether we are close to home or far away. It could be a pocketbook or a stuffed animal or a blanket (something many children carry).

As we get older, we often carry transitional objects, although we may not label them as such. Some people bring things in their suitcases when they travel to set up in the new places they go – a photograph, a ceramic heart, a special stone. And some of us carry our lives in our pocketbooks or purses or backpacks so a part of where we come from is always with us.

Transitional objects know no size or shape or color, but they are tied to our hearts and help us navigate as we enter and travel through an ever-changing difficult world.

Questions to ask of children (and oneself) about the story itself, the history of pocketbooks and the themes running throughout the story.

Questions about the Story

Was the main character of the story older when the story was written? How do you know?

Why was she teased when she was young?

Did what the main character carried in her purse change over time?

How does the main character feel when she thinks she has lost her pocketbook?

Does she worry about her granddaughter being teased?

What is the meaning of the message she leaves in her granddaughter's pocketbook?

General Questions

Do you carry a pocketbook?

What is in it?

Does it go everywhere with you?

How would you feel if you left home without it?

How would you feel if it got lost and was never found?

How would you feel if it got lost and then was found?

Draw your pocketbook or purse or backpack.

Color in or paint the outlined pocketbooks in the story.

Historical Inquiries

What is the origin of the term "pocketbooks?" See:
https://womensmuseum.wordpress.com/2017/05/31/the-history-of-the-handbag/

When were purses/pocketbooks invented?
See: https://www.loveyourleather.ca/leather-blog/history-of-purses/

What is the difference between a pocketbook and a purse, if any?
See: https://steelhorseleather.com/blogs/the-journal/definition-pocketbook?
gclid=Cj0KCQjwgYSTBhDKARIsAB8Kuku9mi2jajhEwtYSm1hAssdgHs0L4IM4qf03Xijwai7Apg8TR
VYR2qYaAnh6EALw_wcB

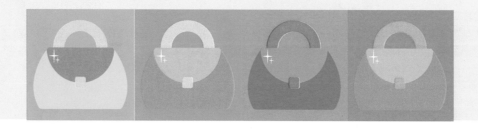

Centuries ago, were purses used by men and/or women? Did that change over time? Do we have prejudice if men as opposed to women carry purses? See: https://getbaggizmo.com/why-are-manbags-so-popular/ and

https://handbags.lovetoknow.com/types-purses/men-purses-from-celebrities-modern-guys and

https://i-d.vice.com/en_uk/article/qvgg87/how-the-handbag-became-gender-neutral

Many books (with photographs) have been written about purses/pocketbooks/handbags. Review one of them and share what you learned from the book.

About the Authors

Susanne Demetri is a retired religious educator who has also volunteered at nursing homes in Massachusetts. She is the inspiration for this story. Some of the pocketbooks featured in this story were illustrated by her granddaughter, Mabel.

Karen Gross is an author, educator and artist who specializes in trauma and has written both adult and children's books. She has also painted some of the pocketbooks in the story.

Sue and Karen are next door neighbors and consider themselves soul sisters who were meant to find each other and did.

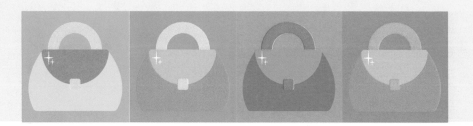

Acknowledgements

This book is available in an audio version that has been produced in partnership with Insight for the Blind - so that all may read. To learn more about Insight or to support their mission, visit www.insightfortheblind.org.

Narrated by Wendy Sager Pomerantz
Edited and Produced by Matt Corey

CPSIA information can be obtained
at www.ICGtesting.com
Printed in the USA
BVRC101011050722
641301BV00003B/15